D0759885

Troupe, Thomas Kingsley,
Military robots /
[2018]
33305240993943
sa   03/09/18

MILITARY ROBOTS

THOMAS KINGSLEY TROUPE

WORLD BOOK

This World Book edition of *Military Robots*
is published by agreement between
Black Rabbit Books and World Book, Inc.
© 2018 Black Rabbit Books,
2140 Howard Dr. West,
North Mankato, MN 56003 U.S.A.
World Book, Inc.,
180 North LaSalle St., Suite 900,
Chicago, IL 60601 U.S.A.

All rights reserved. No part of this book may be reproduced in any
form without written permission from the publisher.

Marysa Storm, editor; Grant Gould, interior designer; Michael Sellner,
cover designer; Omay Ayres, photo researcher

Library of Congress Control Number: 2016050036

ISBN: 978-0-7166-9332-1

Printed in the United States at CG Book Printers,
North Mankato, Minnesota, 56003. 3/17

Image Credits
Alamy: dpa picture alliance, 22; PJF
Military Collection, 28; Premraj K.P., 21;
Stocktrek Images, Inc., 14–15; army.mil: Sgt.
Jason Dangel, 11; US Army, Cover; commons.wiki-
media.org: André Völzke, 4–5; Bwmoll3 / United States
Air Force, 9 (global hawk); Jjamwal, 23; Mark.murphy, 9
(wheelbarrow); Torana, 9 (lightning bug); darpa.mil: Defense
Advanced Research Project Agency, 24 (Atlas); defense.gov:
Lance Cpl. Julien Rodarte, 6 (soldier); en.wikipedia.org: baku13,
8 (Goliath); Greg Goebe, 9 (Aquila); http://news.gc.ca/; Canadian
Armed Forces, 18; iStock: geirrosset, 1; Nerthuz, 31; marforpac.
marines.mil: Lance Cpl. Julien Rodarte, 6 (robot); marines.mil:
Lance Cpl. Abbey Perria, 16–17; marines.mil/Photos: Unknown,
9; Newscom: MICHAEL REYNOLDS/EPA, 26–27; nrl.navy.mil:
US Naval Research Laboratory, 8; Shutterstock: Andrey VP,
3, Back Cover; daseaford, 32; Michal Sanca, 24; Paul Fleet,
8–9; US Airforce / en.wikipedia.org: Master Sgt. Michael
Ammons, 12–13
Every effort has been made to contact copyright
holders for material reproduced in this book.
Any omissions will be rectified in subse-
quent printings if notice is given
to the publisher.

CONTENTS

CHAPTER 1

ROBOTS

to the Rescue

The sound of gunfire fills the street. Bullets whiz through the air. Enemies shoot at a group of soldiers. But the soldiers can't fight back. They are out of bullets. They need help.

Suddenly, something appears in the sky. It looks like a small helicopter. The machine flies above the battle. It delivers **ammo** to the soldiers.

Wired Warfare

Militaries want to keep their soldiers safe. They want to make soldiers' jobs easier. They use robots to help them. Some bots fight. Others bring soldiers supplies. Many help **defuse** bombs.

One fighting bot is the Gremlin. It has a 50-**caliber** gun. Soldiers control where the bot goes. They tell it when and where to shoot.

HISTORY OF MILITARY ROBOTS

Early robots paved the way for the military bots of today.

1923
Electric Dog
three-wheeled machine used to test radio controls

1895

1898
radio-controlled boat
small boat that moved across water and flashed lights

1942
Goliath
remote-controlled mini-tank filled with explosives

1964
Ryan Model 147 Lightning Bug
drone used to take pictures

1979
Aquila
drone created to find enemy targets

2002
PackBot EOD
finds and shuts down bombs

2005

1998
Global Hawk
drone that gathers information

1972
Wheelbarrow
bot that moved car bombs

CHAPTER 2

ROBOTS
in the Sky

Many militaries use robots in the sky. Drones are remote-controlled aircraft. Soldiers don't ride in them. Instead, they guide them from the ground. Built-in cameras show soldiers where the drones fly.

Soldiers fly drones over enemy **territory**. Some drones gather information. Others attack. Attack drones use **sensors** to find targets. They then drop bombs or fire **missiles**.

Because of their size, drones are difficult to see on **radar**.

Benefits of Drones

There are many reasons militaries use drones. Drones are smaller than fighter jets. They are cheaper to build too. Drones are also safer for soldiers. If a drone is shot down, no lives are lost.

U.S. Air Force's MQ-9 Reaper Drone

By the Numbers

12.5 feet
(4 meters)
height

300 MILES
(483 kilometers)
per hour
TOP SPEED

66 feet (20 m) wingspan

10,500 pounds (4,763 kilograms) maximum weight

36 feet (11 m) length

CHAPTER 3

Bomb
ROBOTS

Bombs are incredibly dangerous. They are easily hidden too. To keep people safe, soldiers use robots. From far away, soldiers guide bots to bombs. Soldiers then use the bots to shut down the bombs.

Explosive Situations

The tEODor is a powerful bomb bot. Instead of wheels, it travels on tanklike tracks. The tracks help the bot travel over rough land. It can even climb stairs. The tool at the end of its arm is changeable. Wire cutters, window breakers, and grippers can all be attached.

The tEODor can lift up to 220 pounds (100 kg). It is strong enough to move cars.

Daksh

Another mighty bomb bot is the Daksh. Like the tEODor, it uses **X-ray** to find bombs. It also has a water jet. The jet sprays bombs with water. The water stops them from going off.

• • • • • • • • • • • • • • • • ▶

The Daksh has a shotgun. It can shoot locks off doors.

THE BOMB SQUAD

tEODor

CAMERAS

GRIPPER

TRACKS

Daksh

CAMERAS

WHEELS

WATER JET

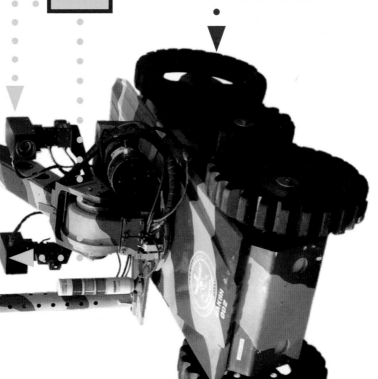

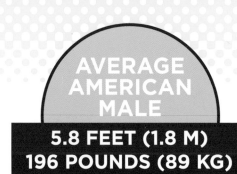

AVERAGE AMERICAN MALE

5.8 FEET (1.8 M)
196 POUNDS (89 KG)

ATLAS
(2ND GENERATION)

5.75 FEET (1.75 M)
180 POUNDS (82 KG)

6 FEET

5 FEET

4 FEET

3 FEET

2 FEET

1 FOOT

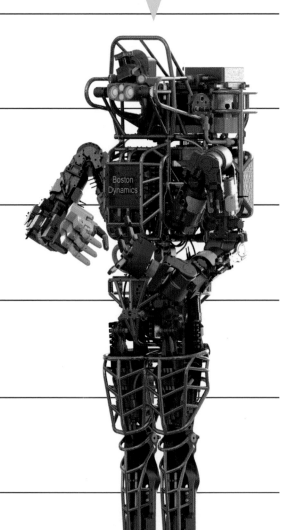

Boston Dynamics

CHAPTER 4

The Future of Military ROBOTS

Scientists continue to make new robots. Atlas is a human-shaped bot. It can walk across rough ground without falling over. The bot can also climb. It also uses tools made for humans. People are still working on Atlas. But someday, Atlas or similar bots could help soldiers on the battlefield.

Robo Sally

Future bomb bots will be
humanlike too. Robo Sally has
arms and hands. A soldier will wear
gloves that control the bot. When
the soldier's fingers move, so will
Sally's. A headset will let soldiers
see what Sally sees.

Working Together

Military bots are very helpful, and they keep improving. The number of robots in the military will continue to rise. During battles and emergencies, robots and humans will work together.

GLOSSARY

ammo (AM-oh)—short for ammunition; ammo is objects fired from guns.

caliber (KAL-uh-ber)—a measurement of the width of a bullet or a gun barrel

defuse (duh-FYOOZ)—to remove the part of a bomb that makes it explode

generation (jen-uh-REY-shuhn)—a type or class of objects usually developed from an earlier type

missile (MIS-uhl)—a weapon that can be thrown or projected to hit an object far away

radar (RAY-dar)—a device that sends out radio waves for finding the location and speed of a moving object

sensor (SEN-sor)—a device that finds heat, light, sound, motion, or other things

shotgun (SHAHT-gun)—a shoulder weapon with a smooth barrel used for firing at short ranges

territory (TER-i-tawr-ee)—an area of land that belongs to or is controlled by a government

X-ray (EKS-rey)—powerful, invisible rays that can pass through objects and make it possible to see inside things

BOOKS

Faust, Daniel R. *Military and Police Robots.* Robots and Robotics. New York: PowerKids Press, 2016.

Mooney, Carla. *Awesome Military Robots.* Ready for Military Action. Minneapolis: Core Library, an imprint of Abdo Publishing, 2015.

Swanson, Jennifer. *National Geographic Kids. Everything Robotics: All the Robotic Photos, Facts, and Fun!* Everything Series. Washington, D.C.: National Geographic, 2016.

WEBSITES

Robotics
kidsahead.com/subjects/1-robotics

Robotics: Facts
idahoptv.org/sciencetrek/topics/robots/facts.cfm

Robots for Kids
www.sciencekids.co.nz/robots.html

INDEX